Open Windows

Selections from the winners of
Poetry in the Windows
1995–2003

translated into the languages of Los Angeles

Edited by Suzanne Lummis

A project of the
Arroyo Arts Collective

First Edition 2005
Published by The Arroyo Arts Collective
P.O. Box 50835
York Station, Highland Park
California 90050-0835

The Arroyo Arts Collective is a grassroots organization of artists, writers and performers formed in 1989 to develop and present creative events that educate and expand the cultural audience in Northeast Los Angeles, one of Los Angeles' most multicultural, and underserved, communities. The many neighborhoods of the Northeast Highlands have rich cultural traditions and the Arroyo Arts Collective strives to link the creative community to the community as a whole by encouraging collaboration that reveals and celebrates the past, present and possible futures of Northeast Los Angeles.

Acknowledgments

Richard Beban's poem, "The Psychiatrist, Narcissus, Writes Up His Findings on Jekyll & Hyde," appears in his book, *What The Heart Weighs*, Red Hen Press, 2005.

Dinah Berland's poem, "Dark Child," was published in *Crania: A Literary/Arts Magazine* (online) in 1999.

Tina Demirdjian's poem, "Pilgrimage to the Hills Above Dodger Stadium," appeared as "Above Dodger Stadium," in her book, *Imprint*, California: Abril Publishing, 2003.

Olivia Friedman's poem, "Heiress to the Laundromat," appeared in *Poetry International*, San Diego State University Press, Issue 9, 2005.

Richard Garcia's poem, "His Wife Folded," appeared in his book, *Rancho Notorious*, BOA Editions Limited, 2001.

liz gonzalez's poem, "I Love Walking West with You," was published in *ArtLife*, Vol. 2, Number 6 in 2002.

Jessica Goodheart's poem, "Earthquake Season," appeared in the *Cider Press Review*.

Kaaren Kitchell's poem, "Earthly Mirabai," appeared in her book, *The Minotaur Dance*, published by Spout Graphic Press in 2003.

Ron Koertge's poem, "Molly is Asked," appeared in *Life on the Edge of the Continent* (University of Arkansas Press).

Deborah Landau's poem, "August in West Hollywood," appeared in her book, *Orchidelerium* (Anhinga Press 2004), as part of a longer sequence called "Lola and The Grape."

Carol Lem's poem, "Office Hour," was published in *The Seattle Review*, Spring/Summer 1996.

Jeffrey McDaniel's poem, "Absence," first appeared in *The Foregiveness Parade*, published by Manic D Press, 1998.

Leslie Monsour's poem, "Parking Lot," will appear in her new book from Red Hen Press, *The Alarming Beauty of the Sky*, to be published early in 2005.

Jim Natal's poem, "Rest Area," appeared in his book, *Talking Back to the Rocks*, Archer Books, 2003.

Sherman Pearl's poem, "Driving Through Cuba," appeared in *Working Papers*, Pacific Writers Press, 1999.

Aleida Rodríguez's poem, "Jacaranda," appeared in her collection, *Garden of Exile* (Sarabande Books), selected as best new book of poetry by the PEN Center USA, © Aleida Rodríguez.

Cherry Jean Vasconcellos' poem, "Stoplight—6th & Alvarado," was published in *Poetry/LA*, Number 16, Spring / Summer 1988.

Charles Harper Webb's poem, "Tenderness in Men" appeared in *Liver*, winner of the 1999 Felix Pollak Prize in Poetry, and published by the University of Wisconsin Press, © 1999 by Charles Harper Webb.

Jackson Wheeler's poem, "Emmaus," appeared in the *MacGuffin*, and was selected for an Honorable Mention by Molly Peacock.

Terry Wolverton's poem, "Cement Dress," was previously published as "i'm in a cement dress" in *Black Slip*, Clothespin Fever Press, 1992. © Terry Wolverton, 1990. Reprinted with permission of the author.

Open Windows is dedicated
to the memory of Diane Alexander,
Co-founder of the Arroyo Arts Collective.

Diane believed that the arts
could revitalize Highland Park.

Contents

Poetry In The Windows I

Poetry In The Windows II

Poetry in the Windows III

Poetry—From Windows to the Page

Who knew?

Every other year since 1995 poems on posters have sprung up in the storefront windows of little shops lining the northern end of Figueroa where it runs through Highland Park—one poem apiece for Bird Man Pet Shop, Mr. Moe Barber, Owl Drug Store, Launderland and Mr. T's Bowl. It's usually during the month of May—the month after National Poetry Month, just to be different—that customers of Happy Day Clothing or El Pavo Bakery can pause for a moment before a winning entry from the Arroyo Arts Collective's Poetry in the Windows contest.

The answer is: not many. Not many people knew. A city as big as Los Angeles has ways of keeping its secrets; it tucks them into its far corners, like Highland Park, Northeast L.A. But many of those who come and go in this Spanish, English, Korean, Vietnamese, Farsi speaking neighborhood knew.

And of course the poets of Los Angeles knew. My selection from five years of first place and honorable mentions includes many of the city's best-known poets—and some of national reputation—along with the recently emerged. We have here a lively sampler of the Los Angeles poetry monde—one that can serve, also, to help prepare new readers for what to expect from contemporary American poetry in general. Though many of these poems could have risen from anywhere, accumulatively they seem to carry a sense of place—that is, they seem to inhabit the language and circumstance of this region, these times. Piecemeal, and in the zigzaggy way of poems by multiple authors, they bring forth a sort of story about a city and its people.

The nature of this contest did require some parameters. Usually the judges—three for each year—took care to select poems that were reasonably short, clear, and versatile enough to stand in either Dr. Vasquez Dentist or West Coast Fragrance as pleasing but not jarring surprises. A new "Howl" won't be found between these covers, nor "The Waste Land," and definitely not the next *Beowolf*. And yet, to its very considerable credit, the Poetry in the Windows contest, dreamed up by The Arroyo Arts Collective's Suzanne Siegel, is the only public art project I know of that does not rise up on neutral ground but goes on faith that each year small merchants will allow poems to be placed within their own domains.

The first year one merchant exclaimed in confusion and dismay when Suzanne walked in and placed a poster in his window. Of course she'd received consent from him earlier but now it seemed perhaps he hadn't understood. He didn't speak English. Braving his protestations and "No, no!'s" Suzanne took him out on the street and urged him to read the words standing in his window—the version translated into his language. And he did. A large delighted smile came over his face. The poster stayed, and every year after he welcomed the new poem selected for his shop.

That first year, too, some shop owners gave the posters to customers who'd asked for them, and had to be instructed that these things must stay up in the windows the full month then be returned to the Arroyo Arts Collective. The year following one shop owner reported that her daughter had so loved the poem she'd copied it down in her journal.

And of folks on the street?—besides, that is, those already predisposed people who drive to Highland Park for the poetry walking tour the first day? I myself can relate only one striking encounter. I think it was the fourth year, somewhere between Mr. Maury's Shoes and 99 Cents Plus. A Latino man, who looked to be about the right age for Occidental College, ran up to me, "This is fantastic! You guys are amazing! I've been reading the poems everywhere. Thank you, thank you for this!"

I asked him if he had one of our brochures with selections of poetry we make available for all the shops. "Yes, yes," he assured me, "I've got everything. This is amazing." I assumed he must be an avid reader. "Have you been interested in poetry for very long?" He answered, still a little out of breath, "Not till today."

No representatives from the city or any funding organization were in my walking tour group that afternoon, and I was glad—because who among them would have believed this? Every once in a while the world conveys to us something too perfect to be real, but it is.

And those other shoppers and passersby who, in alternate years, pause for a time before the windows of Highland Park, come away with more than fresh baked loaves or new pairs of shoes—they receive an exposure to contemporary poetry that puts them above the curve. This according to the National Arts Endowment's recent survey on reading habits in America indicating most citizens don't read any poetry in an average year.

But let the still hopeful NEA representatives call again, now, to you, Reader, who is in possession of this book. You could make a surprising answer to their inquiry, as opposed to the boring ordinary one, the standard, "No, no poetry."

And should someone present you with the question Who knew? you can say Well, I did.

᭣ **Suzanne Lummis**
Editor, *Open Windows*
Highland Park, Los Angeles, 2005

Poetry in the Windows I

Terry Wolverton

Cement Dress

I'm in a cement dress and I can't dance.
I'm in a steel smile and I bite hard.
I'm snorting daggers and I can't breathe.

I'm driving too fast. The morning won't tell me
any secrets. The radio's drained of its last song
and the soft crackle left behind sets this desert ablaze.

I'm running. There are footsteps behind and a
hot wind on the back of my neck. The
birds have scattered and the sky drops slowly.

There are stories I can never tell you. That skyscraper
is about to break across my back. I'm carrying the weight
of the city in my brain. A freeway burns along my spine.

I itch all over. My spiked shoes ricochet
through an empty room. The wind has died. Its sting remains.

I'm in a truth-telling mood and you won't like it.

Vestido de cemento

Estoy en un vestido de cemento y no puedo bailar.
Estoy acorazado dentro de una sonrisa en una mordida aguda.
Estoy bufando puñales y no puedo respirar.

Estoy manejando a gran velocidad. La mañana no me cuenta
sus secretos. El radio se ha secado de canciones
y los susurros que quedan dejan el desierto en llamas.

Estoy corriendo. Hay pasos que me siguen
y un viento caluroso sopla atras de mi cuello. Los parajos
se han dispersado y el cielo está cayendo despaciosamente.

Hay historias que nunca podre contarte. Ese rascacielo
esta por romperse sobre mi espalda. Cargo en mi cerebro la pesadez
de la cuidad. Una autopista arde a lo larga de mi espina.

Me pica el cuerpo. Mis tacones de aguja resuenal
en un cuarto vacío. El viento ha muerto. Queda punzando.

Continúo diciendo verdades que no te van a gustar.

Translation: Pat Alderete

Cherry Jean Vasconcellos

Stoplight—6th and Alvarado

Wings of angels
before my eyes.
Drive through soft
curve and murmur of wings
that open and close,
that sweep my face
finer than breath.
More real than the pick-up
behind me, brighter than the red
and green I try to obey. One
soars in my lap.
Another folds his wings
and cartwheels
on the dash.
My 74 Dodge is filled with angels
who tell me something
I can't quite catch,
something I must remember.
No matter the engine
that knocks, the lady running
for the blind bus,
the boy who sells oranges.
Stop and
deal with the angels.
Stroke the crescent
all the way down.
Rest your head on the wing
of an angel.
Listen for the message
inside the car.

天使的翅膀
顯在我眼簾.
略過柔和的
彎曲和輕語的翅膀
忽關忽開
輕撫我臉龐
輕如鼻息
真實遊邈超過提昇
在我身邊, 比紅更紅
然而綠光我試著服從. 一旅
翱翔在我膝前
再一展翅摺疊
如大風轉
在逶順間
我七四年的道奇老車載滿了天使
有人提及, 事件
我無法撲捉,
但是我必須記得
無論它的引擎
是否敲擊, 女士跟隨
盲車,
一個賣橘子的男孩.
停下
與天使妥協.
輕撫著半月
直洩地面
你頭依天使的翅膀
靜聽細語
輕飄車窗外.

Translation: Rosa Zee

Maurya Simon

Alligator Shoes

Little crocodiles, these shoes
snap at the fishy feet of strangers.
Keep your distance, they say
with leathery tongues.

Still, we're approached constantly
by fish mongers' wives wielding
angry frying pans, by poachers,
by a man from Saks Fifth Avenue
armed with a silk net.

At night my shoes weep and weep;
by day, they lash their tails like whips.
At midnight they quiver on the shelf,
sniffing the scent of rabbit and squid.

They drool shamelessly over cockroaches,
leaving little salty pools on the floor.
I can't take them anywhere anymore—
they hiss when I wear them.

They force me to draw baths for them,
refusing to come up for air.
My life is being ruined
by a pair of reptilian shoes.

And they're not even that comfortable.
But if I refuse to wear them,
they stalk my toes, smacking their lips.
They devour my best wool socks.

But I'm not complaining:
vanity got me into this mess.
Someday, I'll leave them—and
the house, the car, crates of caviar—

I'd like to see them make it on their own.

Zapatos De Cocodrilo

Pequeños cocodrilos, estos zapatos
chasquean los dientes contra los escurridizos pies de los extraños.
Guarden su distancia, dicen,
con sus lenguas curtidas.

Y aun así, constantemente somos asediados
por las esposas de los pescaderos que enarbolan
sus sartenes iracundas, por los cazadores furtivos,
por un hombre del Saks de la Quinta Avenida
armado con su red de seda.

Por la noche mis zapatos lloran que te lloran;
durante el dia sus colas como látigos azotan.
A medianoche se estremecen en su repisa,
olisqueando el rastro del conejo y del calamar.

Por cada cucaracha andan babeando sin vergüenza
dejando charquitos salados en el piso.
Ya no puedo más llevarlos a ningún lado—
pues se ponen a sisear si me los pongo.

Me forzan a llenarles la bañera
y luego se rehusan a subir a tomar aire.
Mi vida está siendo arruinada
por un par de zapatos reptilianos.

Y no es que sean siquiera así de confortables,
pero si me niego a usarlos
se ponen a acechar los dedos de mis pies, chasqueando los labios.
Se devoran mis mejores calcetines de lana.

Pero no me estoy quejando:
fue la vanidad que me metió en este apuro.
Algún día los dejaré; así como a
la casa el carro, las cajas de caviar.

Ya los quiero ver si así sin mí salen al paso.

Translation: León García Garagarza

Joan Probst

International Pork Fat Fever

I want:
chicharrones dipped in salsa verde,
country style ribs, cornbread,
cabbage cooked in salt port and onion.
Gorditas stuffed with carnitas
cooked all night long so you wake up
at four am and smell the sound of hot pork fat.
Baby back ribs dripping
sweet molasses barbecue sauce
torn apart and sucked clean.
Bacon, tomato and mayonnaise
With lettuce slipping out the side
of white bread soft in the middle.
Sausage patty style with biscuits and country gravy.
Pigs in a blanket thick with real maple syrup.
I need:
Italian sausage with green peppers, red peppers, garlic, onion.
Ham hocks. Pigs feet.
Chinese stuffed dumplings, steamed or fried.
Japanese gyoza with vinegar and ginger, soy and chile oil.
Thai pork double fried with garlic.
Pork chops with mustard caper sauce with sour cream.
Give me:
bacon in the salad.
Fried with the greens.
Chile verde. Pork shank.
Easter ham topped with cloves.
Canadian bacon and eggs with wheat, white, or rye toast.
I dream:
of Grandma's sauerkraut and pork roast.
Only Pork.
Knockwurst.
Only Pork.
Chorizo.
Only Pork.

Fiebre internacional de grasa de puerco

Yo quiero:
Chicharrones ahogados en salsa verde,
costillas campiranas, pan de elote,
col cocida en puerco salado y encebollado.
Gorditas rellenas de carnitas
cocinadas a trasnoche para que te levantes
a las cuatro am y huelas el sonido de la grasa caliente de puerco.
Costillas de lomo de cuinito escurriendo
salsa de barbacoa en melaza dulce
desgarradas y chupadas hasta el hueso.
Tocino, jitomate y mayonesa
con lengua a punto de salirse por un lado
del pan blanco suave en medio.
Tortita de salchicha con bizcochos y caldo rústico.
Marranos en una sábana espesa con miel de maple de a de veras.
Necesito:
Salchichón italiano con pimientos verdes, pimientos rojos, ajo, cebolla.
Jarretes de jamón. Manitas de puerco.
Empanadas chinas rellenas, al vapor o fritas.
Gyoza japones con vinagre y gengibre, soya y aceite de chile.
Puerco tailandés doble, frito en ajo.
Chuletas de puerco en salsa de alcaparras y mostaza con crema agria.
Dénme:
Tocino en la ensalada.
Frito con las verdures.
Chile verde. Pierna de puerco.
Jamón de Pascua cubierto de clavo.
Tocino candiense y huevo con tostadas de trigo, centeno o de pan blanco.
Sueño:
con el Sauerkraut y el rostizado de puerco de la Abuela.
Puro puerco.
Knockwurst.
Puro puerco.
Chorizo.
Puro Puerco.

Translation: León García Garagarza

Leslie Monsour

Parking Lot

It's true that billboard silhouettes and power
Lines rebuke dusk's fair and fragile fire,
As those who go on living have to prowl
And watch for someone leaving down each aisle.
While this takes place, a tender moon dips toward
The peach and blood horizon, pale, ignored.

I try to memorize impermanence:
The strange, alarming beauty of this sky,
The white moon's path, the twilight's deep, blue eye.
I want to stay till everything makes sense.
But oily-footed pigeons flap and chase—
A red Camaro flushes them apart,
Pulling up and waiting for my space;
It glistens, mean and earthly, like a heart.

Estacionamiento

Se puede ver que carteleras y alambres
Regañan el crepúsculo, su fuego frágil y hermoso,
Y los seres sobrevivientes tienen que rondar
Entre los pasillos, buscando un lugar vacío.
Mientras tanto, una luna tierna se baja hacia
El horizonte de durazno y sangre, pálida, ignorada.

Yo quiero aprender de memoria lo que no es permanente:
La belleza extraña y alarmante de este cielo,
El sendero de la blanca luna, el profundo ojo azul del anochecer.
Quisiera quedarme hasta que todo sea entendido.
Pero los pichones de patas aceitosas, aletean y se corren—
Un Camaro rojo los divida.
Parándose, espera mi lugar,
Resplandeciendo, tacaño y terrenal, como un corazón.

Translation: Leslie Monsour

Carol Lem

Office Hour

My student says he wrote a poem
about me, but not as I am, not
this tired maestra talking to the blackboard
deafened by the echo of her own voice
but as a poet playing her bamboo flute
on a hill. My student, a Chicano, is sitting
in my office, his eyes focused
on shelves of books, "Do you read all these?"
I don't say these are only textbooks,
my real books are at home, nor do I name
all the poets I love. He can take in
only a few now—Baca, Soto, Rodriguez.
The fluorescent lights above us
hum a broken tune, something like
"America the Beautiful" or "Time on My Hands".
It is late. Everyone has gone home
to shore up their other lives, and East L.A.
is quiet again. What a dream—
a teacher and student meeting at the edge
of a battle zone where drivebys and tortillas,
quinceañeras and someone's mijito cycling a future
on bloodstained sidewalks go on.
"I want to write," he says, "but I can't leave
my turf." I don't say you won't
even when you're a thousand miles from here.
What a dream—a young Chicano
crosses the border to me, a Chinese,
three decades away, to give me a poem,
knowing we are both Americans with a song
to pass on, even if it's still out of tune.
We hear the music in the attention of this hour.
What a dream—When I drove home
the 10 East was jammed with trucks and exhaust
and the San Gabriel mountains a vague vision.
That hill will have to stay in a poem
for a while. But think, without
the blaring horns and broken glass, without
these messages of hope spread across my desk
and the shadow who fills the barrel
of this pen, I could have missed it all.

Horas de oficina

Mi alumno dice que escribió un poema
sobre mí, más no de cómo soy, no
sobre esta maestra fatigada que le habla al pizarrón
ensordecida por el eco de su propia voz,
sino acerca de la poeta tocando su flauta de bambú
en la colina. Mi alumno, un chicano, está sentado
en mi oficina, sus ojos repasan
los estantes de los libros. "¿A poco lees todos estos?"
No le digo que estos son sólo libros de texto,
que mis libros de a de veras están en casa, ni le nombro
a todos los poetas que amo y quiero. Ahora él sólo
podría con unos cuantos—Baca, Soto, Rodriguez.
Sobre nosotros las luces fluorescentes
murmuran una tonada quebradiza, algo asi como
"America the Beautiful" o *"El tiempo está en mis manos"*.
Es tarde. Todo mundo se ha ido a casa
a contener sus otras vidas, *East L. A.*
está sereno otra vez. Qué ensueño—
una maestra y su estudiante encontrándose
en el filo de una zona de batalla, donde las
balaceras y las tortillas, las quinceañeras
y el mijito de alguien en bicicleta circulando un futuro
por banquetas ensangrentadas, siguen su marcha.
"Yo quiero escribir"—dice él—"pero no puedo abandonar
mi territorio." No le digo no lo harás
aunque estés a mil kilómetros de aquí.
Qué ensueño—un joven chicano
cruza la frontera hasta mí, mujer de China,
tres décadas aparte, para darme un poema
a sabiendas que ambos somos Americanos con un canto
que heredar, aunque esté todavía desafinado.
Escuchamos la música en la atención de esta hora.
Qué ensueño—cuando iba a mi casa manejando,
la 10 Este venía congestionada de camiones y humo exhausto
y las montañas de San Gabriel eran una vaga vision.
Aquella colina tendrá que quedarse en un poema
por un tiempo. Pero piensa, sin
las bocinas vociferantes y los vidrios rotos, sin
estos mensajes de esperanza esparcidos a lo ancho de mi mesa
y la sombra que llena el calibre
de esta pluma, pude habérmelo perdido todo.

Translation: León García Garagarza

Poetry in the Windows II

Charles Harper Webb

Tenderness in Men

It is like plum custard at the heart of a steel girder,
cool malted milk in a hot bowling ball.

It's glimpsed sometimes when a man coos to a puppy.
If his wife moves softly, it may flutter like a hermit thrush

into the bedroom, and pipe its pure, warbling tune.
Comment, though, and it's a moray jerking back into its cave.

My dad taught me to hide tenderness like my "tallywacker"—
not to want or accept it from other men. All I can do

for a friend in agony is turn my eyes and, pretending
to clap him on the back, brace up his carapace with mine.

So, when you lean across the table and extend your hand,
your brown eyes wanting only good for me, it's no wonder

my own eyes glow and swell too big for their sockets
as, in my brain, dry gullies start to flow.

Paglalambíng Ng Mga Lalaki

Tulad ng latik sa kaibuturan ng barakilang bakal,
ng malamig-lamig na gatas sa nagbabagang bola ng bolilyo.

Naaaninag minsan 'pag sinusuyo n'ya ang isang tuta.
Sa mahinhing galaw ng asawa'y baka pumagaypáy tulad ng pipit

papasók sa silid at ihuni ang tumataginting n'yang awit.
Ngunit pansinin at isa itong palos na biglang bumabalik sa kanyang lungga.

Tinuruan ako ni tatay na ilihim ang lambing tulad ng pagtatago ng aking "pipito"—
na huwag naisin o tanggapín ito mula sa iba pang mga lalaki. Tangi kong magagawa

para sa nagdurusang kaibigan ay ibaling aking mga mata at, magkunwaring
tatapikin siya sa balikat, bigkisin ang aming mga talukap.

Kaya sa paghilig mo sa hapag, at pag-aabot ng iyong kamay,
sa pangungusap ng iyong mga matang kabutihan ko ang hangad, hindi nakapagtataka

na mga mata ko'y magningning at halos lumuwa,
habang sa utak ko, ang mga barangkang tigang ay magsimulang dumaloy.

Translation: Evangeline Ganaden and Melissa Roxas

Aleida Rodríguez

Jacaranda

The sun comes through the front window,
sits on the little wrought-iron bench
covered in burnt-sugar sculptured velvet,

and I'm old enough to know it will sit like this
only once.
      In the darkened living room my face shines

from the reflection off the fabric and a book that's there—
a monograph on early California plein air painting—
but the amber light seems to flow from me instead,

the way the jacaranda this time of year
blooms so furiously it creates a double on the pavement,
a girl in a summer dress who has walked away from the rest,

stands foot-to-foot with the other girl
upside down in the lake, and it's hard to tell at first
which way is up, which is the true one, which

tossed the violet blossoms—that hover, like confetti,
          only briefly, just this once,
        before they drop—
and which girl perishes, which remains.

Jacaranda

El sol entra por la ventana de enfrente,
se sienta en el banquito de hiero forjado
cubierto por un terciopelo de color azucar quemada,

y yo soy bastante mayor para saber que se sentará así
sólo una vez.
　　　　　En la sala oscurecida mi rostro brilla

con el reflejo de la tela y un libro que está ahí—
una monografía sobre pintura *plein air* de la antigua California—
pero en cambio la luz ámbar parece fluir de mí,

la manera en que la jacaranda a esta altura del año
florece con tanta furia que crea un doblete en el pavimento,
una niña con un vestido de verano que se ha alejado de los demás,

se para unida por los pies a la otra niña
al revés en el lago, y es difícil decir al principio
cuál es la de arriba, cuál es la verdadera, cuál

tiró las flores de color violeta—que quedan suspendidas como confeti
　　　　　　　　　sólo brevemente, esta sola vez
　　　　　　　　　antes de caer—
y cuál niña perece, cuál permanece.

Translation: Aleida Rodríguez

Ron Koertge

Molly is Asked

to be in the Christmas pageant. She tells me
this standing in the door of what we
laughingly call my study.

"But I don't want to be Mary," she says.
"I want to be the guy."

That makes me look up from my bills.
"Joseph?"

"The Innkeeper, I want to slam the door
in Joseph's face."

She's eight. I wonder if we'll look back
on this in a few years and laugh. Or will she
want to be Herod then and we'll have to take
her little brother and flee.

Inimbitahan Si Molly

na lumahok sa palabas para sa Pasko. Sinabi niya sa akin
ito habang nakatayo sa may pinto
ng pabirong tinatawag namin na aking silid-aralan.

"Pero ayokong maging si Maria," ang sabi niya.
"Gusto kong ako ang lalaki."

Napatingin tuloy ako habang inaasikaso ko ang aking bayarin.
"Si Jose?"

"Yung tagapag-alaga ng bahay-paupahan. Gusto kong isara nang malakas ang pinto
sa mukha ni Jose."

Siya ay walong taong gulang. Hindi ko alam kung maaalala namin ito
sa darating na mga taon at magtatawanan kami. O sa bandang huli baka gusto niyang
maging si Herodes, at mapilitan tuloy kaming kunin
ang kaniyang batang kapatid na lalaki at tumakas.

Translation: Evangeline Ganaden and Melissa Roxas

Richard Garcia

His Wife Folded

A man folded his wife into three sections, put them in his
pocket and went walking by the sea. He touched her with his
hand, which he kept in his pocket.

Occasionally he would take her out and hold her to his face, as
if he were studying a picture from his wallet. Was the man
cruel? No, he had often heard her say that she wanted to be
something small that he carried in his pocket.

The wife thought that being folded into three sections was like
having sisters, like looking at herself in a mirror with three
panels—true mirrors, not false ones that turn everything
backward.

As the sun was setting, the man took his wife out of his pocket.
He built a little mound of sand. He scooped out a moat around
it and placed her on top like three cards on a table.

Sitting on the beach this way, his wife remembered her
childhood by the lake: wet sand in her fist, cold then warm; her
tin bucket, blue with big white stars; her yellow shovel, its
serious heft when she pried at the sand. A playfulness of foam
touched her ankles like the lacy hem of a gigantic skirt. She
could sit there forever.

Aware that she was in a private reverie, the man walked farther
down the beach. He brought her here often, although he
disliked the ocean. It was, as he once said to his wife, "too big."
Perhaps next time he would place her in an envelope...address
it to himself. She would like that.

Su esposa, doblada

Un hombre dobló a su esposa en tres secciones, puso estas en su bolsillo y se fue a caminar junto al mar. Las iba tocando con su mano, que tambien guardaba en el bolsillo.

De vez en cuando sacaba a la mujer y la sostenía frente a su rostro, como si estudiara una de las fotografias de su cartera. ¿Se trataba de un hombre cruel? No, pues a menudo él la habia oido a ella mencionandole que muy bien le hubiera gustado ser un objeto pequeñito, que él pudiera llevar consigo en el bolsillo.

La esposa pensaba que el hecho de estar doblada en tres secciones era como tener hermanas. Como contemplarse a sí misma en un espejo de tres paneles. En espejos verdaderos, no en esos espejos falsos que reflejan todo al revés.

Cuando el sol se iba poniendo el hombre sacó a su esposa del bolsillo. Hizo un montecito de arena, cavó un foso alrededor de este y puso a su mujer encima, como a tres cartas sobre una mesa.

Estando así sentada en la playa, la esposa recordó su propia niñez junto al lago: la arena húmeda en su puño, primero fria y luego tibia; su cubeta de hojalata, azul con estrellas blancas; su pala amarilla, el sorpresivo peso que esta adquiría al introducirla en la arena. La espuma juguetona tocaba sus tobillos como el dobladillo bordado de una falda gigantesca. Con gusto se hubiera quedado ahi sentada para siempre.

Conciente de que ella estaba absorta en una ensoñacion secreta, el hombre siguió caminando por la playa. A menudo la traía aqui, a pesar de que el oceáno le disgustaba. Era, como él le dijo una vez a su esposa, "demasiado grande". Tal vez la próxima ocasión él la pondría en un sobre postal … remitido a él mismo. Eso sí que le encantaría a ella.

Translation: León García Garagarza

Carol Colin

Sleeper

I slept through the death of Jesus Rios.
Ted heard the shots, sat up in the dark,
listened for more. A car may have sped off
but nothing else. We sleep with the air conditioner fan
on year-round, to mask the noise of traffic and gunfire,
so I couldn't say if there's been a lot of gunfire lately,
late at night, when the bars get out, when the cars
race by. We do it on purpose so we can
sleep the few hours we need. But it's hard
to believe, when the shots went off maybe forty
feet away, and Jesus caught them
in the gut or chest or head and probably made some
kind of sound, I slept on.
His assailant, his shooter held
the gun still in one or two hands and saw what he had
accomplished. Did *he* make a sound, say anything?
Did he grimace, did he grin? Did his heart race?
Skin grow cold with perspiration? How does that
feel to see Jesus drop and slump and curl in
the quiet Sunday morning? Was there any motive,
any personal reason, some transgression of Jesus'
against this other guy? Or was he taken surprised,
innocent, just because he was there
as they drove up to the corner, the red light.
Should I try to find out? Was he a gangster
living next door? We not knowing, smiling as we
walked past his yard to the store. Either way,
should I take one of these roses Dianne gave us,
add it to his cardboard sidewalk altar
with those of the mothers and girls and children
who go by to the store, stop to read the memorial notes,
study the photo of Jesus' smiling face.

Dormilona

Dormí mientras Jesús Ríos murió.
Ted oyó los balazos, se sentó en la oscuridad,
esperando. Talvez un carro salió pelado
pero nada más. Dormimos con el ventilador
todo el año, para enmascarar el ruido de tráfico
y tiroteo, así que yo no pudiera decir si bien noche ha habido
mucho tiroteo ultimamente, cuando los bares se cierran,
cuando salen pelados los carros. Lo hacemos a propósito para poder
dormir las pocas horas que necesitamos. Pero es difícil
creer, que cuando los balazos se oyeron a unos cuantos metros
y Jesús los recibió
en la panza o el pecho o la cabeza y probablemente hizo algún
tipo de sonido, yo seguí durmiendo.
Su asaltante, su tirador mantenía
la pistola inmóvil en una o dos manos y vió lo
que logró. ¿Hizo algún sonido, dijo algo?
¿Hizo una mueca, sonrió? ¿Se le alborotó el corazón?
¿Se enfrió de sudor su piel? ¿Cómo se
siente ver a Jesús caer y hundirse y enrollarse en
la madrugada de un domingo silencioso? ¿Hubo algún motivo,
alguna razón personal, alguna transgresión de Jesús
en contra del otro tipo? O fue tomado desprevinido,
inocente, solo porque él estaba alli,
mientras ellos manejaban hacia la esquina, la luz roja?
¿Debería tratar de averiguar? ¿Era un pandillero
viviendo alado? Sin saber nada, sonriamos mientras
pasabamos su jardín camino a la tienda. De todos modos,
¿Deberí yo llevar una de estas rosas que nos dio Dianne,
y añadirla a su altar de cartón en la cerra
con las otras de las madres, las amigas y los niños
que pasan camino a la tienda, se detienen a leer notas memoriales,
y estudiar la foto con la cara sonriente de Jesús.

Translation: Alicia Vogl Sáenz

Dinah Berland

Dark Child

Salvadoran soccer players kick a checkered ball
across Los Angeles grass, their red and purple socks
flashing past chain link until the forward knocks
the ball into the goal—close call
for Los Rojos, victors in this pocket park
at dusk with sirens and dogs wailing in shrill
dissonance, the smell of kerosene rising from a grill
the way it did when you were young and knew the dark
streets were forbidden, as you watched the sky
ripen and bleed like the stain of a red-hearted plum
and longed to mount your three-speed bike, to fly
over suburban curbs toward the thrum
of the city, singing a foreign song
until no one could tell where you belonged.

Niña morena

Los futbolistas salvadoreños patean un balón cuadriculado
a través del césped de Los Angeles, sus calcetas rojo y púrpura
relampaguean más allá de la reja hasta que el delantero pega
un tiro en pleno poste—un tantito
para los Rojos, los victoriosos de este parque de bolsillo
en el crepúsculo de las sirenas y los perros aullando bulliciosos,
disonantes, el olor a kerosene que sube de la parrilla
tal como lo hacía cuando eras niña y bien sabias
que una calle oscura está prohibida, cuando veías al cielo
madurando y sangrando como la mancha del corazón de una ciruela
    roja y tibia
y soñabas con andar sobre tu bicla de tres velocidades para volar
sobre las aceras suburbanas hasta el retumbar de la cuidad,
una cancion extranjera sonando en tu garganta,
hasta el punto en que nadie pudiera figurar
ni tu origen ni tu barrio ni tu raza.

Translation: Léon García Garagarza

Poetry in the Windows III

Alicia Vogl Sáenz

A Daughter's Cure For Lou Gehrig's Disease
For My Mother 1928-1989

Sew you a dress
woven of rose petals
shimmering, your garden in May rain.

Color your hair
dye of pomegranates.
Wash each strand
your muscles return.
I am the opposite of
Delilah

A chamomile sponge bath,
talc powder of yellow butterflies
from Macondo. Dust your
skin until Mauricio Babilonia
floats in your eyes.

Wheelchair left behind
you walk, your legs full
your ankles keep a cumbia beat,
the dress rubs you like a cat,
hint of rose rises,
a loose thread follows you

I pull the thread,
wrap it
around my finger
tight.

Remedio para la esclerosis lateral de una hija
para su mamá 1928-1989

Te coso un vestido
tejido con pétalos de rosa
relucientes, tu jardín en llovizna de Mayo

Te pino el pelo
tinte de granada.
Enjuago cada mechón
vuelven tus músculos.
Yo, lo opuesto de
Dalila.

Un baño con esponja empapada
en té de manzanilla
talco de mariposas amarillas
de Macondo. Polveo tu
piel hasta que Mauricio Babilonia
flota en tus ojos.

Dejas atrás la silla de ruedas
caminas, tus piernas robustas
tus talones marcan ritmo de cumbia,
el vestido te roza como un gato,
aparece un aroma de rosas,
te sigue un hilo suelto

lo jalo,
lo enrollo
fuertemente
en mi dedo índice.

Translation: Alicia Vogl Sáenz

Rose Simeroth

Manzanita

So this is what it is to come from fire:
The wind lifts you with the trembling ash
until you take root in sand
where trunk, branches, twigs—all
climb toward the spiny sun.
At the end, no white blossom,
just red raised up forever.

No cool shelter of green here.
Order has been banished
to the other side of the world.
There, oaks are laid out
in logical procession,
a long hand clears a garden,
makes way for civility
and a flat moon.

But the manzanita's red
speaks its own mind, how it needs
fire to burst, bloom and spread.
This Christ would have understood—
I see him thin and wiry,
brooding on the mountain. I see him
brush against the manzanita,
scattering the branches into tiny points...

I, too, was born in the desert.

Manzanita

Así es que esto es lo que sale del fuego:
El viento te levanta con la trémula ceniza
hasta que te enraizas en la arena
donde tronco, ramas, palos—todo
escala hacia el espinoso sol.
Al final, ningún brote blanco,
solamente un rojo elevado para siempre.

Ningún fresco refugio de verdor aquí.
El orden ha sido exiliado
hasta el otro lado del mundo.
Allá, los robles se despliegan
en lógica procesión,
Una larga mano escombra un jardin,
haciendo campo para el civismo
y una luna plana.

Pero el rojo de la manzanita
tiene sus propias ideas, cómo necesita
fuego para estallar, para florear y expanderse.
Esto bien lo hubiera comprendido Jesucristo—
Ya lo veo, flaco y alambrado,
cavilando en la montaña. Lo veo
rozando la manzanita,
esparciendo sus ramas en puntos diminutos...

Yo también soy criatura del desierto.

Translation: León García Garagarza

Ryan Oba

Through The Floor

Kinjiro has decided the earth is flat—
    and that he, of all people, can see
through the floor.
    He has lined his basement with lead
to sleep without fear of falling.

A long time ago his mother left him
    at the store
for opening a bag of Oreos.

Much later,
    alone in his room, he took
a cookie, twisted off the top, and
was almost sucked
              into the lower stars.

Now he cannot risk a wife,
    so he surrounds himself with cages
full of noisy birds.

He may fall through at any time, and
    only their songs remind him
he can fly.

آزادی از درون زمین

<u>کینجیرو</u> بر این عقیده است که زمین مسطح میباشد

او تنها کسی است که درون زمین را میتواند ببیند

سرتاسر زیرزمین خانه خود را با سرب پوشانده است تا

بتواند با خیال راحت بخوابد

مدتها پیش چون یک پاکت بیسکویت را بدون اجازه در فروشگاه

باز کرده بود، مادرش او را جاگذاشت و دیگر برنگشت

مدتی پیش دولایه یک بیسکویت را باز کرد و شروع کرد

به لیسیدن شیرینی وسط آن . با لیسیدن شیرینی خوشحالی

عجیبی باو دست داد و احساس میکرد که میان ستارگان زندگی میکند

او میترسد که ازدواج کند، بنابرین در اطاق خود چندین پرنده

پر سر و صدا را در قفس به عنوان همنشین انتخاب کرده است .

او هرآن ممکن است که به درون زمین سقوط کند و تنها چه چه

پرندگان باعث میشود که او احساس کند که میتواند پرواز کند.

شعر از: راین اوبا   ترجمه: حمید زاوش و مسعود بهشید   ۱۵ آوریل ۹۹

Translation: Max Behshid

Ellyn Maybe

It Was Like A Date

he held doors open for me
he carried my books
he let me order first
I looked into his eyes
my stomach was a butterfly museum
we got to know each other better
I wondered if I'd see him again
a calendar shed history onto the carpet
we talked about music
silence sat atop the napkin dispensers to absorb the shy ingredients
we sat by a window
we finished each other's exclamations
we walked through centuries to get there
the trees changed seasons
vulnerability—the soup of the minute
we found sunflowers in each other's ears
we crossed the streets our heroes lived on and sung their eternity
there were angels in the salt and pepper shakers
I felt like upside down dancing
more a Chagall bride than a woman
more a woman than usual
of this I realized it resembled love.

Dos iz geven vi a tsuzamentref

di tirn hot er far mir geefnt
di bikher mayne getrogn
er hot mir gelozn bashteln ersht
in zayne oygn hob ikh gekukt
un mayn ineveynik is gevorn a flaterl-muzey
mir hobn zikh bakent beser
kh'hob geklert oyb kh'vel im vider zen
a kalendar hot fargisn di geshikhte afn tepekh
mir hobn geredt vegn muzik
shtilkayt hot arayn gezapt di shemevdikayt fun di servetkes
mir zaynen bay a fenster gezesn
mir hobn dem anderns oysrufn farendikt
mir zaynen durkhgegangen yorhundertn tsu kumen dortn
di beymer hobn gebitn di sezonen
di gringe shpirevdikayt—di zup fun minut
mir hobn gefunen zunroyzn in dem anderns oyern
mir zaynen di gasn ariber vu undzere heldn hobn gelebt
un hobn fun zeyer eybikayt gezungen
melokhim zaynen in zalts un fefer mestlekh geven
kh'hob gefilt vi ikh tants mitn kop kapoyer
mer a Chagall kale vi a froy
mer a froy vi geveynlekh
fun dos hob ikh farshtanen az s'iz enlekh af libe.

Translation: Yakob Basner/Workmen's Circle Arbeter Ring

Deborah Landau

August in West Hollywood

All day I watch the neighbor's boy
paint the side of his house.

He seems to rest so easily on the ladder rungs,
shirtless, lanky-limbed, hips tilting in the sun.

In the morning, I am the house, blueing beneath his brushstrokes,
each rib a shingle, my breast, windowpanes, my waist,

the broad wood planks flattening beneath his brushstrokes,
my shoulders, shutters, lips and eyelashes fluttering eaves.

By four, I'm the roller brush,
turned and turning in his working hands.

Come dusk, I'm the open pail of paint
beside him on the grass—wide-mouthed, emptied.

The neighbor's house breathes in its new skin beneath the streetlamp.
It puts its face to the darkness and does not recognize itself.

Tháng Tư ở West Hollywood

Cả ngày tôi ngắm xem cậu trai hàng xóm
quét sơn vách nhà anh ta.

Cậu tựa cách dễ dàng trên những thanh thang,
thân trần, chân tay gầy guộc, chổng mông trong nắng.

Buổi sáng, tôi là cái nhà, trở màu xanh dưới từng nhát cọ,
ngực tôi, mỗi tấm lợp là sườn, eo lưng tôi, các ô cửa sổ,

những tấm ván rộng phẳng lì dưới từng nhát cọ,
vai tôi, mấy cánh cửa, môi và mí mắt tôi kẽ hốc lô xô.

Xế chiều, tôi là cái cọ lăn,
lăn tròn lăn tròn dưới đôi tay miệt mài của hắn.

Cát bụi đến đây, ta là cái chậu đựng sơn
cạn sạch, miệng trống nằm trên cỏ bên cậu hang xóm.

Ngôi nhà láng giềng hít thở trong làn da mới dưới ánh đèn đường,
Phô mặt mình trong bóng đêm và đâu còn nhận ra mình nữa.

Translation: Buu Tu Chung

49

Jessica Goodheart

Earthquake Season

We can hardly tell anymore
whether the earth's trembling wakes us
or my seismometer heart.

Sometimes your aftershock footsteps
make me cry out. I'm not talking
about anything as trivial as the sun
but the loss of it.

What if I die without you
on the greasy tiles of a Taco Bell
in that radioactive light
where no one ever hopes
to look beautiful?

And yet this morning,
the floor rocked me
gently to the breakfast table
and you were there
with sunlight on the cactus.
And the only death I found
buried deep in the paper
as if beneath the collapse
of a house: a boy not yet fourteen
shot in the neck
under an open sky.

Երկրաշարժի Եղանակ

Մենք դժուար կարող ենք ասել
Թէ երկրի ժաժքն է մեզ արթնացնում
Կամ իմ զգայուն սիրտը:

Պատահած քո ուրթի ծայնի շարժումը
Պատճառ է լինում ես զայրանամ
Ես չեմ խոսում արեի այս ոչ կարեւոր
Մի նիւթի մասին,
Բայց իր կորուստը:

Իսկ եթէ ես առանց քեզ մահանամ
«Թաքո-Բէլի» իւղոտ լաստակի վրայ,
Եւ էլեկտրական լոյսի ճառագայթների տակ
Որտեղ ոչ ոք, միՆչեւ անգամ չի լուսար
գեղեցիկ տեսք ունենալ:

Եւ ապա այս առաւոտ
Յատակը ինձ սողեց
Դէպի նախանձշի սեղանը
Որ դու այնտեղ էիր,
Արեի շողերի հետ փշածադիկի վրայ
Եւ միակ մանը որ ես գտայ
Թաղուծ` օրաթերթի խորքը
Տան աւերակի պէս մի տղայ միՆչեւ անգամ ոչ տասանշորս տարեկան,
Կրակած վզին,
բաց երկնքի տակ:

Translation: Carine Allahverdian

liz gonzalez

I Love Walking West With You

down Broadway Avenue because every red
light means a kiss 'til the cuckoo and
because elevator trips turn into carnival

rides at the Orange Show my sister Cindy
and me lost the 11 silver dollars our
Mama gave us when the Zipper flipped

us screaming phone freaks need to hook-up
to e-mail since the l.d. bill cha-chings your
ATM card limiting our fun funds for

Christmas Eve Cindy and me sniffed
the boxes Mama hid in her closet
where I guessed a Francie, Barbie's

suitcase packed because I'm looking
forward to candy tamales and hearing
you breathe beside me at twilight

Me encanta andar al oesta contigo

por la avenida Broadway porque cada luz
roja significa un beso hasta el cucú y
porque viajes por el ascensor se convierten

en paseos del Orange Show donde mi hermana Cindy
y yo perdimos los 11 dolares de plata nuestra
mamá nos dio cuando El Zipper se voltio

nosotros gritadores chiflados del teléfono necesitamos conectarnos
al correo electrónico desde que la cuenta del l.d. cha-ching
tu tarjeta de ATM limitando nuestros fondos de diversión

en la nochebuena Cindy y yo oleamos
las cajas que mamá escondió en su guardarropa
donde yo adivine un Francie, Barbie

una maleta esta empacada porque estoy anticipando
los tamales dulces y escuchandote
respirar a mi lado en la aurora

Translation: Dorothy Avance and Chantel Zepeda

Michael Datcher

ruth (for a sister poet)

she speaks
winds whirl
honeysuckle and jasmine meet
to ponder
why the air is sweeter
now
amber hues swirl
blue and bluest
before they jump black
then ease back into rustic amber
as the last words
the lucky ones
(they knew her longer)
leave her lips
slowly
a spurned sycamore
leans goodbye
while its lone leaf
willingly leaps to death
crooning
"just to be close to you girl"
the four winds sing background
while escorting the spiraling
lovelorn
to the nape
beneath her ear
it rustles her name
before falling to the grass
ruthless
and dead
next to her last words
(the lucky ones)
forever

ሩት (ለገጣሚዋ እህት)

ካንደበቷ ኃይል
የነፋስ አዙሪት ይነሳና
አበቦች ይገናኛሉ፤ ለውሕደት
ለማስላሰል
ለምን ደስ እንደሚል የአየሩ ቃና
በዚችው ዕለት
ወርቃማ ቀለማት ይለዋወጣሉ
ከሰማያዊ ወደ ደማቅ ሰማያዊ
ወደ ጥቁርነት እያሉ
ደግሞም ሊለወጡ ወደ ዝገታማ ወርቃዊ
የመጨረሻ ቃላቶቿ
እደለኞቹ
(ካወቋት ቆይተዋልና)
ከከንፈሮቿ ሲፈልቁ
በዝግታ
ፍቅር የተነፈገው ዛፍ
ለስንብት ይጠጋል
ብቸኛው ቅጠሉ
ወደ ሞቱ እያዘለለ፤ በደስታ
"ካጠገብሽ ልሁን፤ ፍቅሬ!"
እያለ፤ እያንገራገረ
ነፋሱም ከአራቱ ማዕዘናት
ያጅባል ያንን አዙሪት
ቅጠሉን፤ የፍቅር ጥማተኛውን
ማጅራቷ ላይ ሊያሰፍር
ከጆሮ ግንዱ ስር
ስሟን እንዲጠራ በሹክሹክታ
ሳሩ ላይ ወድቆ፤ ጉዞው እስኪገታ
በቆራጥነት
በፍጹም ሞት
ከመጨረሻ ቃላቶቿ ነን
(ከእድለኞቹ ጋራ)
ለዘላለም

Translation: Kiros Berhane

55

Sandra Cutuli

Caution For Children Crossing
—hand-lettered sign on the back of an ice cream truck

I didn't want that boy down the street
in my poem. All I wanted
was my aunt snipping that last loose thread
on my dress, my mother just closing the clasp
of my grandmother's pearls at my neck,
and my father with his camera, trying
to find me in its frame, to focus, snap
his daughter, sixteen, ready to leave
for her first prom. I wanted us
held there in the small square
of the green lawn, my father telling me
what time he wanted me home
as an ice cream truck passed
chiming Brahms' Lullaby.
Then that boy ran into my poem, unwanted.
He chased his mother with a bright
knife. She slammed door after door
between them. I never knew
who called the police. They angled their car
across the driveway. Its radio crackled.
Its lights whirled, hurled yellow grenades
through the air. Those cops poked that boy
with their questions, prodded his silence,
whispered their warnings.
He stood on the grass at the curb, handcuffed,
sixteen, her *I never wanted you*
still ripping the air.
          I wanted to give that boy change
to buy ice cream. I wanted to give him someone
who'd tell him what time he should be home.
But with that boy in the poem,
it could only end
like this.

Precaucion—Ninos cruzando
    —letrero manuscrito en la parte trasera de un carro de helados

Yo no quería a ese muchachito de la cuadra
en mi poema. Yo nada mas quería
a mi tía cortando un último hilo suelto
en mi vestido, a mi madre apenas cerrando el broche
de las perlas de mi abuela en mi cuello,
y a mi padre con su cámara, tratando
de hallarme en su marco, de enfocar, capturar
a su hija de dieciséis años, lista para salir
a su primer baile de secundaria. Yo quería que estuviéramos
ahi unidos, en la placita
con el pasto verde, con mi padre diciéndome
a qué hora tenía yo que regresar a casa,
cuando en eso pasó un carro de helados
tocando la canción de cuna de Brahms.
Entonces ese niño entró corriendo a mi poema, indeseado.
Perseguía a su mamá con un brillante
cuchillo. Ella azotó puerta tras puerta
entre ellos. Nunca supe quién
llamó a la policía. Pusieron su patrulla
en plena entrada. Su radio tronaba,
sus luces giraban, lanzaron granadas amarillas
por el aire. Esos tiras que pincharon al muchacho
con sus preguntas, que picaron su silencio,
que susurraron sus advertencias.
El se paró sobre el pasto junto a la banqueta, esposado,
dieciséis años, la voz de ella *yo nunca te quise*
seguía lacerando el aire.
                    Yo quise darle cambio a ese muchacho
para que comprara un helado. Yo quise darle a alguien
que le dijera a qué hora tenía que regresar a casa.
Pero con ese muchacho en el poema,
sólo pudo haber un desenlace
como este.

Translation: León García Garagarza

Don "Kingfisher" Campbell

Need Comfort? Try...

to walk in a supermarket
pushing a shopping cart
with store muzak wafting
fluorescent lights buzzing above
could be any major city
in the good ol' familiar US
see those bright friendly
boxes of Tide and All
pyramid families of fruits
rows of Campbell's and Cheetos
the ½ price bakery cart
the Cosmopolitan magazine woman
greeting me at the checkstand
then I'm stepping out
into the pole lamp
lit American Night
Volkswagen Vanagons
Honda Civics
Jeep Cherokees in the parking lot
turn my ignition key to return
to the California stucco apartment
I live in, whistling mindlessly
an American tune from my car radio

after I pull out
another car pulls in

¿Necesita comfort? Intente...

caminar en un supermercado
empujando un carrito de mandada
en la tienda *muzak* flotando en al aire
fosforecentes luces zumbando a lo alto
podría ser en cualquier gran cuidad
siendo tan familiar an EU
ver aquellas amistósamente brillantes
cajas de *Tide* y *All*
familiares pirámides de frescas frutas
hileras de *Campbell's* y *Cheetos*
estantes con repostería a ½ de precio
la revista femenina *Cosmopolitan*
saludándome en la caja registradora
entonces al ir caminando afuera
los postres de luz
que alumbran la noche américana
Volkswagen Vanagons
Honda Civics
Jeep Cherokees en el estacionamiento
conecto mi llave de encendido y regresar
al apartamento de estuco californiano
donde vivo silbando con la mente en blanco
una canción de *America* desde el radio de mi carro

después de que mi carro sale
otro coche entra

Translation: Laura Díaz Campbell

Richard Beban

The Psychiatrist, Narcissus, Writes
Up His Findings on Jekyll & Hyde

It wasn't Mr. Hyde's fault, despite
the biographer's slant. It was
Jekyll. Addicted, he was, to the taste
of remorse. He loved his dram
each morning, ruing his evening's
conduct, but nonetheless feeling
superior to the man he'd become
the night before. We all must feel
superior to someone, why not
ourselves? Why not ourselves
at the center of the universe? Our victims
certainly feel less than *we* do. Besides, it is we
who have fallen from grace, deserving
pity for our broken wings.

Az elmeorvos, Nárcissus följegyzi
Jekyll & Hyde — al kapcsolatos észrevételeit

Az életrajzíró megállapítása ellenére,
ez nem Mr. Hyde hibája volt. Jekyll-é.
Ő volt a bűntudat ízének szenvedélyes
rabja. Minden reggel élvezve
egy korty pálinkát, már feledte is
az előző esti viselkedését,
mindig is önmaga fölé kerekedve.
Mindnyájan fölényben akarunk lenni,
miért ne önmagunk fölött? Miért ne
legyünk mi a világ közepe?
Áldozataink úgyis kevesebbet szenvednek
mint mi magunk. Egyebként is,
mi zuhantunk nagyot, kiérdemelve
a sajnálatot törött szárnyainkért.

Translation: Janos Szaktilla

William Archila

Love Poem

Country of moon and oranges
Country of coffee and bells

Here, your name never appears in the news,
unless men with guns run low
through the streets, their clothes dusty and tattered.

Here, no one speaks of your poets,
their voices smaller than their country,
peeling and scratching the word—the grave.

No one knows el cipitio, the river child,
eating ashes to remember you
from distant corners of the world.

No one knows you around these skyscrapers
and wide boulevards, but I feel you,
a pebble caught in my shoe.

My Coca-Cola country
My Coco country

Keep your tiny veins rooted
in my marrow. Don't break
nor erase this map on my face.

Anytime to be a little one
in your small open hands.

Poema De Amor

País de luna y naranjas
País de café y campanas

Aqui, tu nombre nunca aparece en las noticias,
solamente si hombres con sus armas corren agachados
a través de las calles angostas, la ropa hecha jirones y polvoza.

Aquí, nadie habla de tus poetas
sus voces, más pequeñas que su país,
pelan y arañan la palabra—la tumba.

Nadie conoce al cipitio, el niño del río,
el que come cenizas para recordarte
de los puntos distantes de la tierra.

Nadie sabe de ti por estos rascacielos
y anchos bulevares, pero yo si te siento,
una piedrita adentro de mi zapato

Mi país de Coca-Cola
Mi país de coco

Manten tus venas pequenas enraizadas
en mi médula. No quiebres
o borres este mapa en mi rostro.

A cualquier hora para ser un pulgarcito
en tus manos pequeñas y abiertas.

Translation: J. G. Franco

Jenoyne Adams

Pentecostal

Lemme keep you
in the dry place at the center of my tears
in the edges of my frown
that know you hemmin me into
a little girl's pretty dress
when she turn and turn
I fly in circles around myself
keeping time with sunshine

Lemme keep you in my hands
wave them in your sky
feel you, me—us
floating in the turquoise air
wrapping itself like ribbons around our fingers

In my tongue
that needs to know if faith is ripeness
forgiveness yellow
if hope is passed down in the stitches
of a handmade quilt

If love is the blueberry filling
in my father's homemade pies

If love is the dance that died
in my mother's eyes

If love is silence spoken instead of words

Keep me
when I naked and cannot clothe my spirit in smiles
when pain feels bigger than blessing
family, like a bed of strangers
and you are not the friend I want to talk to

When life is not a circle but a line and I cannot make ends meet

Be the cinnamon sugar in my oatmeal
peppermint drop at the bottom of my purse
solid of my bone and tenderness in the pads of my fingers

Be my everything, even when I forget that you are
and keep me

Pentecostal

Déjame guardarte
en el sitio seco al centro de mis lágrimas
en las orillas de mi ceño
que saben que tú me tejes dentro
del hermoso vestido de una niña pequeñita
cuando ella gira y gira
yo vuelo en círculos alrededor de mí misma
contando el tiempo con el sol

Déjame guardarte en mis manos
agítalas en tu cielo
siéntete, a mí—a nos
flotar en el aire turquesa
que se envuelve en sí como listones en nuestros dedos

En mi lengua
que necesita saber si la fe es madurez
si amarillo es el perdón
si la esperanza ha pasado a las puntadas
de un cobertor hecho a mano

Si el amor es un relleno de zarzamoras
en los pays que mi padre horneaba en casa

Si el amor es la danza que murió
en los ojos de mi madre
si el amor es el silencio que habla en lugar de las palabras

Guárdame
cuando estoy desnuda y no puedo arropar mi espíritu en sonrisas
cuando el dolor se siente más que bendita
la familia, como un lecho de extraños
y tú no eres el amigo con quien yo quisiera hablar

Cuando la vida no es un círculo sino una línea y yo no puedo contenerla

Sé el azucar de canela en mi cereal
la gota de menta en el fondo de mi bolsa
solidez de mi osamenta y ternura en las falanges de mis dedos

Sé mi todo entero, aun cuando yo me olvide que tú eres
y guárdame

Translation: León García Garagarza

Poetry in the Windows IV

Jackson Wheeler

Emmaus

He overtook me on the road to Emmaus
and we walked together discussing

what better path I might have chosen
given the lay of the land, the slope of trail

whether or not the Pass was closed.
He so favored my dead brother,

I could not take my eyes from him
And asked him to supper.

He said yes, and the light, it seemed,
followed us home,

where he sat beside me
until I was certain of who he was;

I then reached for a plate of figs,
turned back to his empty chair.

What did I expect
in that chill autumnal air?

엠마우스

그는 엠마우스로 가는 길 위에서 나를
따라잡았고 우리는 함께 이야길 나누며 걸었다.

주어진 지형이나 길의 경사 등, 내가
선택했을 수도 있는 더 좋은 길에 대하여

그 길이 막혀 있든 아니든간에.
그는 내 죽은 형을 그렇게도 빼어닮았다.

나는 그로부터 눈을 뗄 수가 없었고
그래서 그를 저녁식사에 초대했다.

그는 그러마고 했고, 그리고 빛이, 그렇게
보였다, 집으로 우리를 따라온 것같이,

내 옆에 그가 앉은 곳으로
그가 누군지 나의 확신이 설 때까지;

그리곤 내가 무화과 접시를 집으려다
뒤돌아보니 그의 의자는 비어 있었다.

무엇을 내가 기대했던가
쓸쓸한 가을의 대기 속에서?

Translation: Sung Y. Yi

Sherman Pearl

Driving Through Cuba

My '56 Chevy, all chrome and cool and Turtle Wax—
it might've been salvaged here, fixed
again and again till it aged into one of these
smoking jalopies that cruise the half-empty streets
looking backward, chugging down roads
that fall off the island's edge.
It might've been born here. Who knows,
when it was young and able to take the bumps
it might've joined the revolution,
climbed the Sierra Maestra bearing arms for the rebels;
might've rammed Batista's barricades,
served as Fidel's parade car as he rode through Havana.
Ah, these scrap-heaps keep going, held together
by hairpins and slogans. They seem powered
by the fumes of history. And the past rides on in them,
slumped in the back like a road-weary hitchhiker.
Why, my Chevy might've ended
as one of these cabs that cruise avenidas
named after heroes—Martí, Bolívar, Allende.
I hail them from the crumbling sidewalks with nods,
half-smiles, slow waves.

Cuba en auto

Mi Chevy del '56, puro cromo, cachondo y encerado:
capaz que fue rescatado por estos lugares, reparado
una y otra vez, para envejecer y convertirse en uno de estos
cacharros humeantes que aún andan rolando por las calles semi-vacías,
que van mirando para atrás y van tosiendo a lo largo de las carreteras
que se desparraman al filo de la isla.
Capaz que hasta naciera aquí, quién sabe,
y hasta cuando fuera joven,todavía capaz de andar sobre los topes,
se uniera a la revolución,
trepara la Sierra Maestra llevándole parque a los rebeldes,
anduviera echando carga contra las barricadas de Batista,
sirviérale al mero Fidel de carro triunfal cuando desfilara por La Habana.
Ay, estos pedazos de chatarra que siguen andando
a base de alfileres, saliva y refranes,
como si los echaran a andar las humaredas de la Historia.
Sus pasajeros son los ayeres:
ahí van aplastados en el asiento trasero, como recogidos al aventón.
Mira nomás que mi Chevy pudo haber acabado
como uno de esos taxis que recorren las avenidas
con nombres de héroes: Martí, Bolívar, Allende.
Yo así los aclamo, desde las banquetas agrietadas, a cabezadas los llamo,
con medias sonrisas y ademanes amplios.

Translation: León García Garagarza

Jim Natal

Rest Area

Forest fires raged in Idaho that summer when you pulled off the Interstate
east of Boise, parked, and cut the engine. Your whole body vibrated with

the churn of tires, slipstream of distance spreading like a concrete wake
behind you. The air was thick with char, sky smoke-damaged the orange-gray

of August steel town dusk. You held the wheel, didn't you, as if afraid to
let go, watched plumes rising over ridges of evergreen hills, turned the music

off. A car door unlocked beside you. A woman stood, wary, pistol holstered
on her belt, infant strapped to the front seat, belongings piled in back. You were

faceless, weren't you, simply part of her scan. You walked behind the buildings
for a better view of the fire; when you returned to your truck, she was gone.

You can drive for days in this country, for static-filled nights on end, plotting
the points on a graph of your restlessness—Albuquerque, Salt Lake, Reno, Yuma,

Bakersfield, Spokane, Laramie, Lincoln—assembly line of inter-
changeable destinations, miles strung between like troughs of wires.

Sometimes people stop on these highways, never get back on, hole up,
flickering, in disappeared motels to wait it out, adopt a mutt and a

TV Guide, hotplate dinners and beer cans. Not you. Because
you think you will just keep driving, follow tail lights as if Polaris,

your life held to the right of parallel yellow lines (divided, then broken),
a bird that cannot sleep, its instinct only for migration, pausing

to feed and briefly rest. When there's no arrival, what can leaving mean?
Somewhere the mountains are being consumed; ash is falling like souls.

Aire de Repos

Cet été-là, le feu flambait dans les forêts d'Idaho, lorsque tu es sorti de l'autoroute
à l'est de Boise, tu t'es garé et tu as coupé le moteur. Tout ton corps vibrait ivre de vitesse,

le flot de la distance, s'étendait comme un sillage en beton, derrière toi.
Une forte odeur de brûlée embuait la ville et le ciel, en ce crépuscule d'août, semblait

arder d'une couleur orange-grise. Tu tenais le volant comme si tu avais peur de lâcher, tu
regardais la fumée s'élever au-dessus des collines verdoyantes , et tu as éteint la musique.

La portière d'une voiture s'ouvrit à côté de toi. Une femme se tenait debout, hésitante, un
pistolet à la ceinture, un nourrisson attaché au siege avant, ses affaires empilées derrière.

Tu n'étais qu'un visage anonyme faisant simplement partie de son parcours. Tu allas
derrière les immeubles pour avoir une meilleure vue du feu; quand tu es revenu à ton
camion, elle était partie.

Dans ce pays on peut conduire pendant des jours, durant des nuits sans fin pleines de
parasites, reliant les points de la courbe de ton impatience—Albuquerque, Salt Lake, Reno,
   Yuma,

Bakersfield, Spokane, Laramie, Lincoln—une chaîne de destinations interchangeables
des kilomètres de distance telles les vides entre les poteaux télégraphiques.

Parfois, des gens s'arrêtent sur ces autoroutes, pour ne plus jamais reprendre la route, se
terrant, vacillant, attendant dans des motels perdus, ils prennet un chien et un

Guide Télé pour compagnon, des dîners rechauffés et des canettes de bière. Pas toi.
Parceque tu penses pouvoir continuer à conduire, à suivre les feux arrière comme si

c'était l'Etoile du Nord, ta vie se tenant à droite des lignes jaunes parallèles (divisées
   puis coupées),
tel un oiseau ne pouvant dormir, guidé seulement par son instinct de migration,

s'arrêtant pour manger et se reposer brièvement. Lorsque qu'il n'y a pas d'arrivée, que
   peut partir signifier?
Quelque part les montagnes sont en train d'être flambées; les cendres tombent comme
   des âmes.

Translation: Tara Baban

Majid Naficy

Have You Seen Me?

The old palm
Does not open his mouth
And the playful wind
Has no secret
But the rustling of dry leaves.
In the darkness of night
I open the mailbox
And I stare at the face of a man
Who, one day, was wandering around
In the cold streets of Tehran
And today lives at the end
Of that narrow hall.

نخل پیر زبان نمی گشاید
و باد با زبانش
جز خش‌خش برگها‌ی خشک
رازی ندارد
در تاریکی شب
صندوق نامه را می گشایم
و به چهره‌ی مردی خیره می شوم
که یک روز
در خیابانها‌ی سرد تهران
پرسه می زد
و امروز
در انتها‌ی آن راه‌روی باریک
خانه دارد

Translation: Majid Naficy

Jeffrey McDaniel

Absence

On the scales of desire, your absence weighs more
than someone else's presence, so I say *no thanks*

to the woman who throws her girdle at my feet,
as I drop a postcard in the mailbox and watch it

throb like a blue heart in the dark. Your eyes
are so green—one of your parents must be

part traffic light. We're both self-centered,
but the world revolves around us at the same speed.

Last night I tossed and turned inside a thundercloud.
This morning my sheets were covered in pollen.

I remember the long division of Saturday's
pomegranate, a thousand nebulae in your hair,

as soldiers marched by, dragging big army bags
filled with water balloons, and we passed a lit match,

back and forth, between our lips, under an oak tree
I had absolutely nothing to do with.

あなたがいないということがこんなに重いとは
知りませんでした。たとえどんなに美しい人が
私に身をゆだねようとも私には全く興味が
ありません。あなたのことを考えるだけで
私の胸はときめきます。

あなたの深い緑のひとみ　あなたの髪に
まとわるざくろの花や星くずと私は
覚えてます

かげ木の下で重ねたあなたのやわらかい
くちびると思い出してます

Translation: Junko Nirei and Steve Webb

Kaaren Kitchell

Earthly Mirabai

There are many ways
to be in the world.

My way is mad
with love.

A yellow butterfly
meanders past my house.

Wherever you go
I will follow.

संसारिक मीराबाई

अनेक रीत हैं
दुनियामें रहने के लिये.
मेरी रीत है
इसकसे पागल.
मेरे घरके पास उड़ती फिरती
अेक तितली पीली.
तुम जहाँ जाओगे
मैं चलूँगी पीछे पीछे.

Translation: Margaret Patel

Linda Anne Hoag

Route 66 Love Song

You are the attraction
Of all my roadsides.
Woo me with Philly chicken,
Rocket burgers and Grapette.
Perfume me with maple syrup,
Sagebrush, chili, and oranges.
Plant me a garden of Cadillacs.
Waltz me in a meteor crater.
I come to you with a heart
Tender as frozen custard.
Do not send me alone
Into a cavern filled with outlaws.
Carry me over the threshold
Of your stucco wigwam.
Hold me all night
In your truckdriver arms.

Canción de amor de la Ruta 66

Tú eres la atracción
De todas mis desviaciones.
Sedúceme con pollo estilo Philly,
Hamburguesas Rocket y Grapette.
Perfúmame con miel de maple,
Matas de salvia, chile y naranjas.
Plántame un jardín de Cadillacs.
Baila un vals conmigo
En el cráter de un meteoro.
Yo vengo a tí con el corazón tan tierno
Cual un flan bien congelado.
No me mandes allá sola
A la caverna donde acechan malhechores.
Llévame en tus brazos a través del umbral
De tu wigwam de estuco.
Abrázame toda la noche
Con tus fuertes brazos camioneros.

Translation: León García Garagarza

Stephanie Hemphill

Mother Road

The old route an impacted wisdom tooth
buried beneath new interstates, a road
of lost teeth, the sly grin between Chicago and LA
haunted by the clinks of chipped coffee cups,
rusted out Chevys, the dust mouth of a day
without water, a pickup's black hot engine
coughing to reach the summit, diesel, burger
and human sweat soaked into her pavement.
Grandma Joad's unmarked grave just outside
Newberry Springs. The Mother Road cut
her molars 75 years ago. Now her saucer
of teeth frowns on the countertop. Criminy,
if the day weren't blown-dry hot and the miles
stretched in only one direction, maybe
we'd "find the time holy." This zigzag trail
of American Dream now a busted up bridge
over the Colorado River, a town of withered
gas stations and a boarded up motor court.
Still the old route sings a ditty the new highway
tries to muffle till some old snoop straps her ear
to the asphalt, taps out the beat and plants
the requisite arrows pointing from the salvage yard
in Towanda, IL where we bury our dead to Homer,
CA, the city of none, on her knees for a zip code.
Route 66 rolls her tongue further and further west,
beds her kickstand at the Pacific's pursed lips.

Główna Droga (Ruta 66)

Stara droga to ubity ząb mądrości zakopany pod nowym
międzynarodowym chaiłejem, drogą z zgubionych zębów,
cwany uśmiech pomiędzy *Chicago IL.* i *Los Angeles*,
prześladowany przez dzwonienie szczapowatych,
porozbijanych kubków kawy, zerdzewiałe Chevy, zakurzone
usta dnia bez wody, ciężarówki czarny gorący silnik kaszlący
aby dotrzeć do szczytu, diesel, hamburgery i pot
prezesięknięty do dna podłogi.
Babci *Joad* nieoznaczony grób zaraz na krawędzi *Newberry
Springs*. Ta Pierwsza Droga uciela jej zęby tronowe 75 lat
temu. Teraz jej zębowa podstawka krzywi się na stole. Jejku,
żeby ten dzień nie byl tak wysuszono gorący i te mile nie
ciągnely sie tak w jedną stronę, może wtedy byśmy znaleźli
"czas święty." Ta kręta droga Amerykanskiego Marzenia,
teraz zawalonym mostem nad Rzeką *Colorado*, miasto
zwiedniałych stacji bęzynowych i zakutych zajazdni.
Ale i w dalszym ciągu ta stara droga podśpiewuje to co nowa
jezdnia próbuje uchiszyć do puki jakiś stary ciekawieć nie
umocuje ucha do asfaltu, wybije rytm i zasieje wymagane
strzałki wzkazujące zbiórki odpadków w *Towanda, IL.*
gdzie zakopujemy zmarłych do *Homer, CA.*, miasto nikogo,
na kolanach szukając numer wskazujący.
Ruta 66 odwija swój język dalej i dalej na zachód, kładzie
swój stojak w Pacifiku wypukłych ust.

Translation: Inka Bujalska

Tina Demirdjian

Pilgrimage to the Hills above Dodger Stadium
—In memory of Manazar Gamboa

Again we arrived, the rain pouring into us
like sheets of metal. We trespassed
for your solemnity, standing on a hillside
supple rose petals between our fingers.

God laughed thunder. Your pearl whites
now dust beneath my feet.
At 1:30 p.m.—the sky polished itself.
Rain gods pushed away. The blow-horn
of a gourd raised you in our hands.

Below us, in "La Bishop," you sank deeply
into the wet earth
where you breathed your youth once
and made poems appear before you were ready.

Until you landed in a solitary place, not in the fields,
not near the ocean, not in your bedroom—
in a small cell behind bars. You faced yourself
on pages of white lined paper
and dug deep just like your body did today.

So, my friend—

Today, was not a new experience for you.
You soaked into the earth with your pen
and your eyes, black and Apache. Ancient.

You drove cotton into your hands with your songs
and your sisters'. You dreamt of warriors:
Aztecs and sun gods
placed their hands on you, and from you
a child was born, Olmeca Sol, and a language
so old even the wind recognized it.

And then you were gone between the folds of our skin
something in all of us so old that recognized it, too.

다쳐 스타디움 언덕에의 순례
-마나사 감보아에게 부쳐-

다시 우리는 도착했네, 비가 철판 위처럼 퍼붓는
우리들 손가락 사이에 나긋한
장미꽃잎들이 느껴지는 언덕 위에
우리는 당신의 위엄 속을 가로질러 갔네.

신은 천둥으로 웃었네. 당신은 진주 빛
먼지가 되어 내 발 밑에 있고
오후 1 시 30 분- 하늘은 다시 반짝이는데
우신(雨神)은 밀려 나갔네. 표주박 나팔 소리는
당신을 우리 손안에 일으켰네.

우리들 아래 "교구" 안에, 당신은
젖은 땅 속으로 깊이 가라앉았네. 그곳에서
한 때 젊음이 숨쉬었고
준비되었을 때 보일 시를 지었지.

들녘이 아닌, 바다 근처가 아닌, 당신 침실도 아닌,-
빗장 뒤 조그만 방, 고독한 장소에
도달할 때까지 당신은 하얀 줄이 있는
종잇장 위에서 스스로를 대면했고
오늘 자신의 육신처럼 그렇게 깊이 파들어 갔지.

그러니, 내 친구여-

오늘이 새로운 경험이 아니었네.
당신은 붓과 옛날 아파치의 검은 눈을 가지고
땅 속으로 스며들었네.

당신과 누이, 그 노래를 가지고 숨처럼
손을 부드럽게 하였지. 당신은 용사도 꿈꾸었네:
아즈텍 그리고 태양신들이
그들의 손을 당신 위에 놓았지. 그래서
올메카 솔이란 아이 하나가 태어났지.
그리고 너무 오래되어 바람조차도 알 수 있는 언어도.

그리고 당신은 우리들의 근육
그 주름살 사이로 가 버렸지.

Translation: Sung Y. Yi

Poetry in the Windows V

Sung Y. Yi

The Belt

When I get up in the morning
And buckle up the belt
I am ready.

Though it is only a strip of leather,
It changes our lives as the Serpent
Changed Adam. He went
To look for some clothes.
He put on his belt.
It protects us from shame or cold,
And makes us honorable to the world.

It energizes me like Samson's hair.
The necktie is attractive
But it could be dangerous
And makes me weak and timid
Like a salaried man facing the lay-off.

That hot summer in Seoul,
When meat was in high demand,
A thief butcher pounded
My dog, *Baduk*, for a stew.
He was wearing a collar not a belt.
The animals, including my dog,
Are dominated by humans because
They don't know how to buckle the belt.

In the sixteenth century, my hero Admiral *Yi*
Fought the Japanese for seven years
And lost not a battle. How?
He invented the turtle ship, used superior strategy
And, first of all, for seven years, he never untied
His belt.

허리띠

내가 아침에 일어나서
허리띠를 매었을 때
나는 비로소 채비가 되었다.

비록 그것은 하나의 가죽끈에
불과하지만, 배암이 아담을
바꾼 것처럼 우리의 삶을 바꾼다.
그는 옷을 찾으러 나섰었다.
그리고 허리띠도 매었다.
허리띠는 우리를 부끄러움이나
추위로부터 막아주고 세상에 대해 떳떳하게 한다.

삼손의 머리카락처럼 나를 힘나게도 한다.
넥타이는 매력적이긴 하지만,
위험하고, 해고를 앞둔
봉급쟁이처럼 나를 유약하고
비겁하게 만든다.

그 무덥던 서울의 여름,
개고기 수요가 한창일 때,
어떤 도둑 개백정은 보신탕용으로
나의 개, 바둑이를 끌어갔다.
그 때 개는 허리띠를 매지 않고 목줄을 매었었다.
아마도 개를 포함한 짐승들이
허리띠를 맬 줄 몰라 사람들로부터
지배만을 당하고 사는지도 모른다.

16세기, 나의 영웅 이순신은
7년간의 일본과의 싸움에서
한 번도 패한 적이 없었다. 그 비결?
그는 거북선을 만들었고, 탁월한 전략을 썼지만,
무엇보다 중요한 건, 그 7년 동안,
한 번도 허리띠를 풀은 적이 없었다.

Translation: Sung Y. Yi

89

Cathie Sandstrom

Releasing The Birds

Next to her embroidered lawn handkerchiefs
my mother's empty gloves lay
paired in the nest of her drawer:

short white Easter ones that stopped at the wrist;
netted crocheted gloves for summer; an ecru pair
four inches past her watchband, the backs detailed

with three rows of stitching raised like fine bones;
three-quarter length pigskin to wear under coats;
black lace for cocktails, white for weddings;

sexy gloves with gathers up the length so they'd
look like they were slouching; the knitted
Bavarians, Loden green, stiff as boiled wool.

My first prom dress—strapless, floor-length—I wore
her formal opera gloves. Pearl buttons on the delicate
underside of my wrists, then the white went up and up.

I kept six pairs, my sister took the rest. Saying
someone should use them, she gave them away
at work, set them out for the taking.

Tonight, I lay the table with my mother's china.
At each place, a pair of gloves palms up, wrists
touching in a gesture of receiving and giving.

I held back the gloves she'd bought in Italy: black
leather, elbow length, the right glove torn at thumb
and palm as if she'd reached for something too late

or held onto something too long.

Wypuszczanie Ptaków

Koło jej haftowanych husteczek na trawnik
Leżą puste rękawiczki mojej matki
W parach, w gnieździe jej szuflady

krótkie białe Wielkanocne które zatrzymywały się nad przedgarstkiem
Siatkowo szydełkowane rękawiczki na lato; ekrowa para
cztery centymetcrów za zegarka pas, tyły detalowane

wyszywane w trzy rzędy podniesione jak delikatne ości;
trzy-czwarte w długości skóra wieprzowa do noszenia pod płaszczem;
czarna koronka na koktajle, biała na wesele;

sexowne rękawiczki sciągane na cała długość zeby wygladały jakby
się skórczały; Bawaryiki na drutach,
zieleń Lodenska, sztywne jak gotowana wełna.

Moja pierwsza sukienka balowa, bez ramiączek I aż do podłogi–Założyłam jej
formalne rękawiczi do opery. Perłowe guziczki na delikatnej podłoży moich
przedgarstków, wtedy biało podnosiło się coraz wyżej i wyżej.

Zatrzymałam sześć par, moja siostra wzięła resztę. Mówiąc
że ktośpowinien je urzywać, oddała je w pracy,
wyłozyła na wzięcie.

Dzisiej wieczorem, wyłozyłam stół matki porcelaną.
Na karzdym miejscu, para rękawiczek dłoniami do góry,
przedgarstki dotykając się w geście otrzymania i oddania.

Zatrzymałam czarne rękawiczki które kupiła we Włoszech;
Czarna skóra, do łokiecia, prawa porwana na kciuku i dłoni
jakby sięgała po coś za poźno

czy trzymała coś za długo.

Translation: Inka Bujalska

Lisa Marie Sandoval

Chola Love Song

My baby's father tattoos a title across
our screeching child. I watch
the letters curve, tender and cool,
as they slope clean crests of green,
a crown that will kill him someday.

I mull over the man who sired my son.
Bald as a boy, barely sixteen, he sucked
me through my skin beyond his teeth and
into a world of lewd gangsta laws
promising me freedom from my virgin self.

I listened to his lull. Luring my heart
he cooed in my ear as he discharged
himself into me. Today he pours
a nickname into the neck of our nighttime fling
now two-years-old, soon to be three.

I enfold my baby, cradling him underneath
the skin of my thigh, pinning him to the couch.
His Daddy pens his future below
the bawling skull. My *Lil' Angel* has received
his inheritance, a ready-made life from a father

to his son. *Big Angel* sings the same soothing tune
he crooned to me the evening of our lust. I lost
my head to his homies and was grossed
with pleasures not my own. I can hear still
the yowling now between my knees.

El canto de la chola

El padre de mi baby tatúa un título a
través de nuestro niño chillón. Yo miro
las letras curvándose, tiernas y calientes,
subiendo y bajando como olas limpias y verdes,
una corona que lo matará algún día.

Yo contemplo al hombre quien engendró a mi hijo.
Calvo como una canica, con apenas dieciséis años,
me chupó por mi piel y más allá de sus dientes y a
un mundo de leyes pandilleras prometiéndome
libertad de mi ser virginal.

Yo escuchaba su arrullo. Atrayendo a mi corazón,
él me tarareaba al oído mientras se descargaba
dentro de mí. Hoy se derrama
un apodo a la nuca de nuestra noche amorosa,
ya tiene dos años, y tres pronto tendrá.

Yo envuelvo a mi hijo, acunándolo debajo
de la piel de mi muslo, sosteniéndole sobre el sofa.
Su Daddy dibuja su future abajo en
el cráneo gritándose. Mi *Lil' Angel* ha recibido
su herencia, una vida ya hecha de un padre

a su hijo. *Big Angel* canta la misma melodía
que me arrullaba la noche de nuestra lascivia. Perdí
mi cabeza a sus vatos y fui atacada
por placer que no era mío. Lo puedo oír todavía,
el gran llanto entre mis dos rodillas.

Translation: Lisa Marie Sandoval

Robert Peake

Neruda's Grammar School Crush

He whispers, "*muñeca*" with lips too young
to grow a moustache or quote the manifesto.

While Nicanor was guessing her underwear color,
Pablito saw shells curled in her hair,
spume weeping on caramelized skin,
love that foams and love
that pulls back in deadly undercurrents.

Even then his sad gaze transformed everything.

She waves him goodbye for the summer like seaweed
fluttering over a drowned sailor's cheek.

El amorcito de Neruda en su juventud

Susurra, "muñeca" con labios tan jovenes
que aun no pueden ni cultivar bigotes ni repetir el manifiesto.

Mientras Nicanor adivinaba de ella el color de sus calzones,
Pablito imaginaba conchas en sus rizos,
rocío llorando en piel de azúcar quemada,
amor que hacía espuma, y amor
que fluía en corrientes bajas y mortales.

Aun tan joven, su triste mirada transformó todo.

Ella le dijo adiós con la mano hasta pasar el verano
como alga agitando sobre la mejilla
de un marinero ahogado.

Translation: Ofelia Mancera and Robert Peake

Shahé Mankerian

Chloe Comes Quietly

She has the moon
in her suitcase.
When she's in my room,
she lets it out.

I would like to skip
my sleep and watch
the moon rise.

She stands on my bed,
slices the moon
into half—
I'm exaggerating.

Her fingers play
shadows against the wall.
"Can you see the cat?"
she asks.

And I focus
on the shadows I see,
the Chinese landscape,
the rice fields,

the waterways,
the reeds,
and the moon rising
out of her suitcase.

Պլօին Կու Գայ Գադտնօրէն

Իր պայուսակին մէջ
Լուսին մը կայ։
Երբ սենեակիս մէջ է,
Դուրս կ՚արձակէ զայն։

Կը նախրնտրեմ զանցել
Փունս եւ դիտել
Լուսածագը։

Ան անկողինիս վրայ կենալով
Կը կիսէ լուսինը
Երկուքի––
Կը չափազանցեմ։

Իր մատները կը խաղան
Պատին վրայի շուքերուն հետ։
«Կատո°ւն կը տեսնես»,
Ան հարց կու տայ։

Եւ ես կեդրոնանալով
Շուքերուն երեսը կը տեսնեմ
Ջինական բնանկարը,
Բրինձի դաշտերը,

Ձրանցքները,
Եղեգները,
Եւ լուսնի ծագումը
Իր պայուսակին մէջէն։

Translation: Shahé Mankerian

Olivia Friedman

Heiress To The Laundromat

I come after school to refill the detergent
boxes of bright red and blue and gold painted

like the long candy aisles. I love to watch
the coins rush from the trays like silver

minnows that I try to catch in my fists.
In the evenings my mother steadies

the washing machine while my father
looks inside its hard belly that eats his

face until it goes quiet. He pulls out the long
metal insides, he squeezes and screws as if a baby

was coming out soon. The Mexican
woman with the dark, heavy blankets

she's never done folding, looks and looks
at my father's underwear creep up over his

jeans. All the hard mothers glare
at the baskets we wheel around them

and their small children:
they don't know anything.

They crowd around my thin
sandwich and run up and down

the aisles as if they were not giving
us quarters to wash their dirty socks.

Clothes tumble in big fights and the mothers
sit down on the bench like they've been running

too long. Their hair sticks out in gray wires.
Their breasts are sad and used. Their wallets

are thick with coupons and
quarters and we take them all.

Наследница к "Прачечной"

Я пришла после школы наполнить с мыльным порошком
коробки с яркими красными и голубым и золотым красками

как длинные конфетные аллеи. Я люблю наблюдать
монеты, бегущие с лотков как серебрянная

телюзга, которую я пробую поймать с моими руками.
По вечерам, моя мать устанавливает

стиральную машину, тогда как мой отец
смотрит вовнутрь её твёрдого брюха, которая ест его

лицо, пока она затихнет. Он вытягивает длинные
металлические внутренности, он сжимает и поворачивает
как будто младенец

выйдет оттуда скоро. Мексиканская,
женщина с тёмными, тяжелыми одеялами

она никогда не закончит складывать, смотрит и смотрит
на моего отца нижнее бельё, которое выползло изпод его

штанов. Все крепкие матери пристально смотрели
на корзины мы катили вокруг их

их маленькие дети
они не знают ничего.

Они толпятся вокруг моего тонкого
бутерброда и бегают вверх и вниз

аллей как будто они не дали
нам монеты постирать их грязные носки.

Бельё кувыркается в большой борьбе и матери
сидят на скамье как будто они бежали

очень долго. Ихние волосы торчат как серые провода.
Ихние груди грустные и использованые. Ихние бумажники

плотные с купонами и
монетами и мы забираем всё это.

Translation: Tibi Friedman

Larry Colker

Classified Ads, May 1, 1608

2410 COUPLES THERAPY

Let me not to the marriage of true minds admit impediments. Love is not love.

2570 TAILOR / DRY CLEANER

Which alters when it alteration finds, or bends with the remover to remove; O, no! it is an everfixed mark.

2600 MARINE FORECAST

That looks on tempests and is never shaken; It is the star to every wandering bark.

2780 APPRAISALS

Whose worth's unknown, although his height be taken.

2810 COSMETICS

Love's not Time's fool, though rosy lips and cheeks.

2920 FARM IMPLEMENTS

Within his bending sickle's compass come.

3130 ESCHATOLOGY

Love alters not with his brief hours and weeks, but bears it out even to the edge of doom.

3355 EDITORIAL SERVICES

If this be error and upon me proved, I never writ.

4080 WOMEN SEEKING MEN

Nor no man ever loved.

Mica Publicitate, Mai 1, 1608

2410 **TERAPIE DE CUPLU**

Nu cred în piedici puse de noroc
Unirii sufletelor mari. Iubirea-Iubire

2570 **CROITOR / NUFĂRU**

nu-i când face silei loc,
Trădării răspunzând cu părăsirea.

2600 **SERVICI NAVALE**

Nu, ea e vesnic semn si strājer
Ce-ntâpinā furtuna si nu cade.
E steaua fiecārui corābier,

2780 **EVALUARI DE PREȚ**

Al cārei pret nu-i māsurat in grade.

2810 **TEATRU DE PĂPUȘI**

Iubirea nu-i paiata vremii, chiar

2920 **ANTICHITĂȚI**

De intrā sub compasul coasei sale,

3130 **POETRE DE MORMÂNT**

N-o schimbā ani, si n-o clintesc
mācarTāisurile clipelor fatale

3355 **AVOCAT**

De spun minciuni, si pot fi dovedit,
N-am scris nimic,

4080 **FEMEI CĂTÎND BĂRBARȚI**

si nimeni n-a iubit!

Translation: Ion Frunzetti and Lucian Plesea

Mary Armstrong

The Edge

Six of us in Louie's Ford head north on Alvarado,
past the hospital, past the midnight dreariness
of storefronts, steel gutters ticking with the start of rain.
Streets slick, we turn and skid at corners;
our faces shine and fade as we pass streetlights,
signals, race up a hill to reach the top, where
Louie lets the engine idle. "Come on," we yell, "let's go."

This is what we came for: the drop into the dark,
the long, steep slide before we lift in air
as if we're weightless; flying. Then, the jolt
of earth on axle, the spin into the chain-linked yard
of Mrs. Apodaca who, awakened, hammers Louie
with her shoe, promises him early death, forgetting
how desire can take you to the edge, eager
for what lies ahead; laughing, racing toward it.

El Filo

Seis de nosotros en el Ford de Louie rumbo norte en Alvarado,
pasando el hospital, pasando la pesadumbre que la medianoche
pone en las fachadas de las tiendas, los desagües de acero
resuenan con la llegada de la lluvia.
las calles resbalan, damos vuelta y nos derrapamos en las esquinas;
nuestros rostros resplandecen y se borran según pasamos los faroles,
los semáforos. Carrereamos cuesta arriba hasta la cima, adonde
Louie deja el motor andando. "¡Ándale!"—gritamos—"¡Vámonos!"

Para esto venimos: la caída en la oscuridad,
la larga y empinada resbaladilla antes de levantarnos por los aires,
como ingrávidos; volando. Luego, el golpe
de la tierra contra el eje, la voltereta hasta el patio enrejado
de Doña Apodaca quien, despertada, martillea a Louie
con su zapato, prometiéndole una muerte pronta, olvidando
cómo el deseo te lleva hasta el filo, ansioso
por lo que vendrá adelante; riendo, corriendo para allá.

Translation: León García Garagarza

Merchants Acknowledgment

Of the more than forty-five businesses that have participated in Poetry in the Windows projects, fifteen displayed poem posters for all five projects over the last ten years: Folliero's Pizza, Highland Park Shoe Repair, West Coast Fragrance, Owl Drug Store, Century 21, Mr. Moe Barber, Quick'r Print'r, Marcello's Hair Salon, The Sewing Center, Random Gallery, Arroyo Furniture, Catalina's Bridal Shop, Highland Park Florist, Frank's Camera and Modern Studio of Photography. Sadly, Catalina's Bridal Shop which always displayed a romantic poem, Mr. Moe, one of our most enthusiastic supporters, and Highland Park Shoe Repair, whose Korean speaking owner always received his poem translated into Korean, have gone out of business.

Other merchants displayed posters for Poetry in the Windows more than once. Ralph's Shoe Repair, Odette's Hair Style, Launderland, The Cleaning Lab, Mr. T's Bowl, Hello Kitty / Steele's Gifts, El Pavo Bakery, California Fashion Beauty Supply, Mr. Maury's Shoes, Highland Park Liquor, Bird Man Pet Shop, Meija Travel, El Paso Shoes, L. A. Star Embroidery, Family Clothing and Blind Impressions all participated for several years. The Arroyo Seco Branch of the Los Angeles Public Library was also a venue for poem posters until construction of a new library relocated the facility into temporary quarters.

During the ten years' span of Poetry in the Windows, some businesses closed, changed hands or were transformed into new ventures. People's Department Store became a 99 cents store, Highland Park Hardware became Happy Days Clothing Store, Smokin' Bones Restaurant briefly became Heart and Soul, TV Café became El Huarache Azteca #3 for a short time, and the Collective was sorry to lose an important cultural anchor with the closure of Arroyo Books.

Whether businesses displayed a poem once, as did Arroyo Vista Family Health Center, Dr. Vasquez—Dentist, Meija's Video, 99 Cents Plus, Health Store, Olympic Tae Kwan Doe, or Marti's Party Supplies or for all of the five Poetry in the Windows, the Arroyo Arts Collective deeply appreciates the merchants' support in offering their windows.

꩜ **Suzanne Siegel**
Administrative Coordinator
Poetry in the Windows I-V
Highland Park, Los Angeles, 2005

Workshop Poems

Instuctor's Statement

Visiting Poet at Franklin High School—
Youth Poetry Workshop in conjunction with the Arroyo Arts
Collective's *Open Windows* anthology.

As a teen, I was a closet poet and rhyming about emotions of the soul.
In contrast, this next generation writes about deeper identity issues
and life-and-death themes. Perhaps it is because they have never
lived in a world without the threat of nuclear war, gang violence,
deadly drugs, AIDS, and such stringent laws for beauty where even the
most gorgeous of society require alterations.

I began the workshops performing from my own collection, "The
Yowling & Other Sounds from Highland Park," and told the students
I was interested in how life in our neighborhood looked through
their eyes. Fostering a safe and supportive environment was an
important priority, so during our initial meeting I asked them to
share their personal goals for the workshops. At first these young
poets were shy and unsure that their precious words would mean anything to anyone else. Throughout our time together, they discovered
how to access creativity through brainstorming, how to create a poem,
and the art of revision. Eventually, they left their shyness behind and
learned to share their words aloud, applaud one another, and to give
and receive constructive feedback. The poems that follow are from
the most timid teens of the group.

汆 Lisa Marie Sandoval

Dalia Narvaez

I Am From

I am from the noise of cars,
from much smoke, and people walking fast.
I am from the green, white, and red flag,
I am proud to belong to the Aztec pride.
I am from electricity and technology,
from big buildings and poor ecology;
I am from the poor but happy neighborhood,
where I lived the happiest moments of my childhood.

I am from Guillermo and Priciliana's daughter,
from where the families are very large.
I am from the person, who always prays for me,
I am in the middle of this family tree.
I am from the clean dishes and soft blankets,
from celebrations of birthdays with really big cakes.
I am from delicious tamales, and mole,
where the women know how to cook a good pozole.

I am from the biggest treasure of Juana's life,
from the blood heredities of Bernabe's pride.
I am a construction of bricks and wood;
I am from the great traditions of going to church.
I am from strong arms and really big hearts,
from the serious face with eyes like stars.
I am from old memories and happy days,
from those "I love you honey"s that my father says.

Graciela Lima

Brief Poems

i.
Blur

I am just a blur of what could have been
A ghost of the wildest dream
A walking lie

ii.
Thinking

As I listened to the pictures
The colors told me a poem
And the forms whispered their ideas

iii
Mirage

The image in the mirror
Came out and hugged me
She kissed me and told me
"Everything's fine
On both sides of the glass"

Instuctor's Statement:

**Visiting Poet at Luther Burbank Middle School—
Youth Poetry Workshop in conjunction with the Arroyo Arts
Collective's _Open Windows_ Anthology, with support of
Hathaway Family Resource Center**

In order to fully appreciate the first of Francisco's poems, one
must have a sense of where he started—which is pretty much where
all beginning poets start whatever their ages—with general descrip-
tions and few lively details. Here is the beginning of his first
draft: "...I went to Universal Studios./First I went on the
rides./My first ride was Jurassic Park The Ride./At first it was boring but at the end the ride fell down./Next I went to Revenge of
The Mummy The Ride./At first it was great..."

Francisco assured me it was this visit to Universal Studies he most
wanted to write about but, he said, he could hardly remember the
rides, "it was so long ago—six months ago." I worked with him and
others in my small group of Burbank Middle School students to
help them recover memories already beginning to fade, and—most
importantly—to render these with vivid details and energetic language that would draw readers into their experiences.

Now, to fully appreciate Francisco's second poem one must know
what one can reasonably expect from a boy of that age. My friend
Dan's son is 23 now but once, for a year, he was Francisco's age.
When Dan heard the poem "For My Mother," he asked me the
poet's age. Thinking he'd misheard me, he asked again.
Then..."Eleven?! He's eleven!? What is he, some kind of boy
genius?"

O.K. I helped a bit, but no more than Pound helped Eliot with
"The Waste Land," and no one questions Eliot's authorship. I
asked questions to jog my student poet's memory when he got
stuck, and by suggesting to him that this particular poem would be
beautiful in couplets. But I can take no credit for a quality, a gift,
he simply had with him when he walked in the first day of class—
the determination to see a thing through, and to stick with a poem
until he felt satisfied, until it felt right.

        &ct~~ **Suzanne Lummis**

Francisco Javier Alarcon

The Revenge of the Mummy—The Ride

Here in Los Angeles
my dad sits next to me.
The dark makes me nervous.
I don't know if he's nervous.
What will I feel?
How fast will I go?
It's dark as space without
the stars and sun.
I'm not scared—I like action.
At first we slide
around a curve, then...
Swish!
I feel a fierce wind.
Then
the ride goes down.
I feel my lungs come
out of my stomach.
We speed past
holographic mummies—
orange, green and
yellow lights.
I'm *still* not scared!
I like action.
Then
the ride rewinds
backwards!
Then
my mom and dad,
my little brother Angel,
and me,
go for sushi.

Francisco Javier Alarcon

For My Mother

You're from a place called Guerrero,
with dry hills, cows munching slowly, thirsty trees.

You love planting vegetables in the back yard—
guayavas—like lemons but sweet and juicy.

Every afternoon when you come back from work
you water the lemon tree with a hose.

You harvest chilies red and green as the colors
of the Mexican flag.

You taught me the verb *to water*.
I help you *regar* the roses and chilies.

You love to grow—from seeds and little parts
of big plants, because you come from a dry land.

Arroyo Arts Collective Acknowledgments

The publication of *Open Windows* would not have been possible without the help of many dedicated people. The Arroyo Arts Collective is indebted to all the poets who participated in the five Poetry in the Windows projects. Each year of Poetry in the Windows brought submissions from over a hundred poets. We are grateful for such a heartfelt outpouring of poetry. We are thankful, too, for the many volunteers who translated poems into more than twenty languages. For all five Poetry in the Windows we were fortunate to have established poets who served as jurors. They spent countless hours reading the submissions and choosing the very best. Many thanks to Jorge-Mario Cabrera, Suzanne Lummis, and Russell Leong in 1995; Carol Lem, Bill Mohr, and Alicia Vogl Sáenz in 1997; Erin Aubry Kaplan, Richard Garcia, and Cherry Jean Vasconcellos in 1999; Robert Arroyo, Jr., Laurel Ann Bogen, and Rubén Martinez in 2001; and Paul Lieber, Pireeni Sundaralingam, and Jackson Wheeler in 2003.

Although the merchants along Figueroa have been mentioned earlier, we cannot say enough about the generosity of all those who opened their windows to poetry.

The Collective also thanks *Open Windows'* Editor, Suzanne Lummis, who has been onboard since the first Poetry In The Windows as a champion of poetry and poets in Los Angeles, our Project Director, Linda Anne Hoag, Youth Workshop Leaders, Suzanne Lummis and Lisa Marie Sandoval, Book Designer, Cidne Hart, Illustrator, Carol Colin and Letterpress artists, Carl and Lynn Heinz of The Backyard Press who designed and printed the cover. Suzanne Siegel, who was Administrative Coordinator for all five Poetry in the Windows' projects offered invaluable help in putting the anthology together, as did Laurie Arroyo, stalwart Co-President of the Arroyo Arts Collective. Joan H. Ramirez was undaunted by the formidable task of typing and organizing the poems and translations. All the board members of the Arroyo Arts Collective offered assistance and encouragement throughout the long task of putting the anthology together. We thank the Westcott Press for making the Collective's first book a reality.

Poetry in the Windows I-V were supported by generous grants from the Lannan Foundation, the National Endowment for the Arts and the City of Los Angeles, Cultural Affairs Department. Additional assistance was given by the Highland Park Chamber of Commerce and the Automobile Club of Southern California.

Open Windows is made possible by a generous grant from the City of Los Angeles, Cultural Affairs Department.

Book design, Cidne Hart. Illustrations, Carol Colin. Cover, Carl and Lynn Heinz.